A Note to Parents and Teachers

Eyewitness Readers is a compelling new reading programme for children. *Eyewitness* has become the most trusted name in illustrated books, and this new series combines the highly visual *Eyewitness* approach with engaging, easy-to-read stories. Each *Eyewitness Reader* is guaranteed to capture a child's interest wh. developing his or her reading skills, general knowledge and love of reading.

The books are written by leading children's authors and are designed in conjunction with literacy experts, including Cliff Moon M.Ed., Honorary Fellow of the University of Reading. Cliff Moon spent many years as a teacher and teacher educator specializing in reading. He has written more than 140 books for children and teachers, and he reviews regularly for teachers' journals.

The four levels of *Eyewitness Readers* are aimed at different reading abilities, enabling you to choose the books that are exactly right for each child.

Level 1 – Beginning to read
Level 2 – Beginning to read alone
Level 3 – Reading alone
Level 4 – Proficient readers

The "normal" age at which a child begins to read can be anywhere from three to eight years old, so these levels are only guidelines.

No matter which level you select, you can be sure that you're helping children learn to read then read to learn!

www.dk.com

Editor Sheila Hanly
Art Editor Jill Plank
Senior Editor Linda Esposito
Senior Art Editor Diane Thistlethwaite
Cover Designer Margherita Gianni
Production Melanie Dowland
Picture Researcher Cynthia Frazer
Illustrator Peter Dennis
Natural History Consultant
Theresa Greenaway

Reading Consultant
Cliff Moon, M.Ed.

Published in Great Britain by
Dorling Kindersley Limited
9 Henrietta Street
London WC2E 8PS

2 4 6 8 10 9 7 5 3 1

Eyewitness Readers™ is a trademark of
Dorling Kindersley Limited, London.

Copyright © 1999 Dorling Kindersley Limited, London

A CIP catalogue record for this book is
available from the British Library.

ISBN 0-7513-598-82

Colour reproduction by Colourscan, Singapore
Printed and bound in Belgium by Proost

The publisher would like to thank the following for their kind
permission to reproduce their photographs:
Key: t=top, a=above, b=below, l=left, r=right, c=centre

Bruce Coleman Ltd: Kim Taylor 43 crb; **Environmental Picture Library:** Herbert
Girardet 40–41; **Mary Evans Picture Library:** 8 bl, 10 cl, 12 clb, 42 tl; **Robert Harding
Picture Library:** 37 tr, **James Webb/Phototake NYC:** 24 cl; **Image Bank:** 14–15;
Image Quest: Peter Parks 26 cl; **Kobal Collection:** 16 cla, 39 cr; **Moorfields Eye
Hospital:** 4 tl, 30 cl; **Oxford Scientific Films:** 6 tl, 14 c, 18 tl, 19 tr, 22 tl, 22 cla, 36 br,
36 bl, 37 bl, 38 tl; **Science Photo Library:** Alfred Pasieka 44 cl, Andrew Syred 38–39,
Astrid & Hanns-Frieder Michler 36 cla, **CNRI:** 9 b, David Scharf Front Jacket, Back
Jacket, 22–23, Dr. H. C. Robinson 16 cr, Dr. Jeremy Burgess 7, Dr. Jeremy Burgess 19 cr,
Dr. Kari Lounatmaa 44 crb, Dr. P. Marazzi 6 b, 29 cra, **Eye of Science:** Front Jacket, 33
b, J. C. Revy 10 br, 14 tl, John Burbidge 12 tl, K. H. Kjeldsen Front Jacket, 17, 18–19,
London School of Hygiene 41 tr, Mark Clarke 9 tr, Michael Abbey 39 tr, Microfield
Scientific Ltd Front Jacket, Rosenfeld Images Ltd 29 crb, St. Bartholomew's Hospital 11 br;
The Wellcome Trust: 40 cl.

The publisher would also like to thank
Frank Greenaway and Andy Crawford for additional photography, the Medical
Entomology Centre, Cambridge for supplying bed bugs for photography, and
Rachael Parfitt for allowing her dog, Daisy, to appear in the book.

Contents

EYEWITNESS READERS

PROFICIENT
4
READERS

MICRO MONSTERS
LIFE UNDER THE MICROSCOPE

Written by Christopher Maynard

DK

London • New York • Sydney • Delhi

It's a bug's world

Mite fright
Some scientists think that about 90% of adult humans have tiny mites living at the base of their eyelashes.

Meet Christopher Maynard – our host. We depend on him to stay alive. He provides us with warmth, food, and shelter.

Who are we? Most of us are so tiny you would need a microscope to see us properly. We are the army of tiny creatures that live on, around, and even inside Christopher's body.

I am a head louse, sucking blood from Christopher's head. Read about me on pages 6–13.

Christopher is feeling awful. That's because millions of us streptococci bacteria are growing in his throat. You can read about us on pages 44–45.

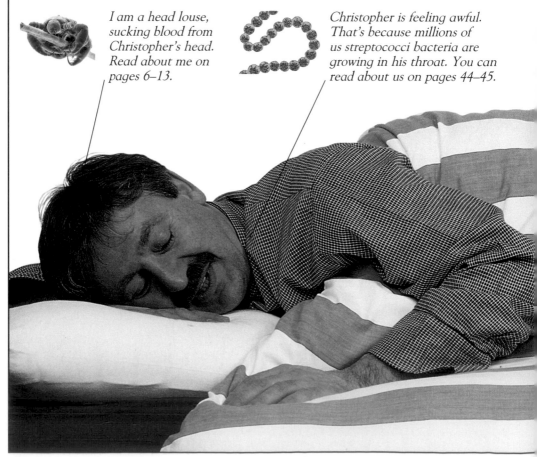

We shelter in his hair, feast on his skin and tunnel into his body. And there are billions more of us who don't live on Christopher …

In the pages of this book you will see lots of close-up photographs of the tiny creatures that live on you and in the world around you. You can meet us face to face and read all about us – in our own words.

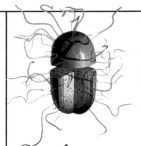

Countless
Your body contains about 100,000 billion bacteria. But don't bother trying to count them – they are too small to see.

I am one of more than a million dust mites living in this quilt, eating Christopher's dead skin flakes. Read about me on pages 26–27.

I am a flea. I've just bitten Christopher's dog. Read about me and my family on pages 14–21.

When I feel hungry, all I have to do is crawl down the hair shaft to the scalp. It's a little like you raiding the refrigerator for a snack. I push out my long mouth parts and poke a tiny hole in the scalp. I spit some saliva into the hole. This makes the blood flow more freely so I can drink it easily and quickly.

Old friends
Lice and humans go way back. Lice remains have even been found in the wrappings of ancient mummies.

Equal rights
As far as head lice are concerned, all humans are equal. Rich or poor, they all make perfectly good homes.

Shaft of human hair

The hooked front legs are just the right size to grip a human hair.

If I bit into your scalp, you would feel a little itchy. That's because my saliva is irritating to human skin. An itchy scalp may be a sign that my friends and I have come to live on your head.

Once I start feeding, I drink until my whole body is filled to bursting with blood. When I've finished my meal, my long mouth parts shrink back into my head. This meal is enough to keep me going for about three hours. I need to feed often. If I get stuck on a hat or a comb, I will soon starve to death.

No kidding
Head lice are more often found on children than adults. This is simply because children's heads are checked for lice more often.

Lice girls
Female head lice develop quickly. They can start to lay their tiny eggs at the age of only eight to nine days.

Big families
Like the old woman who lived in a shoe, a female louse has a huge family. In the two to three weeks that she lives, she lays about 100 eggs.

Tiny tots
Nits are less than 1 mm long. That's about the same size as the head of a pin.

Head lice grow up fast. By the age of eight to nine days, I was fully grown and I had met my mate. Soon after, she began to lay tiny silvery-white oval eggs in special casings called nits. Every night she would lay eight to ten nits.

A young louse hatches out of the egg casing, or nit

She carefully placed each nit on its own shaft of hair, right at the base near the warm scalp. Then she cemented it in place with special waterproof glue. That way, when our human host scratched his head or washed his hair, the nits would not work loose.

For more than two weeks my mate kept laying eggs until she had laid about 100 eggs in all.

As the human's hair grew, the nits were slowly moved away from the scalp that was keeping them warm. The lice inside the nits had to hatch out before they got to the cool zone and died. After eight or nine days, out they came, exact copies of their parents, and able to feed and care for themselves right away.

Lice mystery
On human girls, most nits are found over and behind the ears. On boys, most nits are found on top of the head.

Egg head
If you find a nit more than 12 mm away from your scalp, it will be empty. The louse inside will have hatched.

A rare case – hair with hundreds of nits

Usually no more than ten lice live on one human head. If the head I am living on becomes too crowded, I shall have to move on to another head. I can't fly or jump, so I shall have to wait until another human head touches the head I am living on.

A louse scurries along a hair shaft at top speed.

Then I shall run quickly along the hair shaft and climb onto the other head.

If too many of us stay on this head, our human host will start feeling very itchy. Then he might try to get rid of us. But he won't find it easy to do this. Dunking us under water makes no difference at all. Neither does shampoo or conditioner. We just hang on tightly and hold our breath.

Even anti-lice shampoo doesn't always work on us. The only thing that is certain to do the trick is careful combing with a special fine-toothed comb. It breaks our legs and loosens our tight grip on the hair. After that, it's impossible for us to hang on any longer.

Favourite brand
If one anti-lice shampoo is used too often, lice can become immune to it – you will need to try a different brand.

The louse's mouthparts are tucked away when the louse is on the move.

A tough, leathery outer covering makes the louse hard to crush.

A nit glued onto the base of a hair shaft

13

The flea files

I am a flea. To be precise, I'm a cat flea, although at the moment I'm living on a dog. This isn't a problem as far as I'm concerned. We fleas live on any animal that has a permanent nest or bed, so dogs, cats, rabbits, mice, squirrels and even humans are all good hosts for us.

Fleas and fleas
Cat fleas differ from dog fleas by having a longer snout. You can see this snout only under a microscope.

A rabbit flea feeding in a rabbit's ear

Squashed flat
Fleas' hard bodies are flattened sideways. This helps them to squeeze easily through the hair, fur and feathers of their victims.

I've been living on my dog for several days now, ever since it went to sleep on the thick rug where I hatched out of my cocoon.

As soon as I sensed a warm body nearby I headed straight for it. I was lucky. I landed on a thick, furry coat with my first jump.

I was really hungry. So I slipped down to the skin, bit hard, and took a long drink of blood. My first warm meal made me feel better, although it didn't stop me from wanting to bite my host again. I nip him several times a minute when I'm hungry.

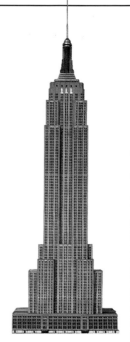

Big jumpers
Fleas can jump almost 30 cm. That's about 130 times their own size.

If humans could jump 130 times their height, they could leap halfway up the Empire State Building.

Biting back
Tiny mites live on fleas and torment them with bites, just as fleas torment us.

A flea has a sharp snout instead of teeth for biting into skin.

Powerful back legs launch the flea into the air as it jumps from host to host.

Bug check
One way to check if a pet has fleas is to brush its coat over damp newspaper. If dark specks fall out and turn the paper pink, your pet has fleas – the specks are the droppings of feasting fleas.

Bloodthirsty
Like the famous vampire Count Dracula, fleas need blood to stay alive. They must drink blood before they are able to lay eggs.

In the next week or two, I'll eat about 15 times my weight in blood. Each time I feed, I'll stab the skin with my sharp snout and suck up a droplet of blood.

Our bites do not bother some hosts at all. But with hosts who are allergic, the saliva we leave in the wounds sets off an itchy skin reaction – a small spot inside a swollen red ring.

Even though two pets might be equally infested, one will scratch and nip like crazy, while the other behaves calmly as if there were not a single flea on it.

When I'm full of blood, I don't stop to digest my meal. Instead, I keep biting my host as hard as ever. This lets me produce lots of droppings of undigested blood. These droppings fall into my host's bed, where they become food for the next generation of growing fleas.

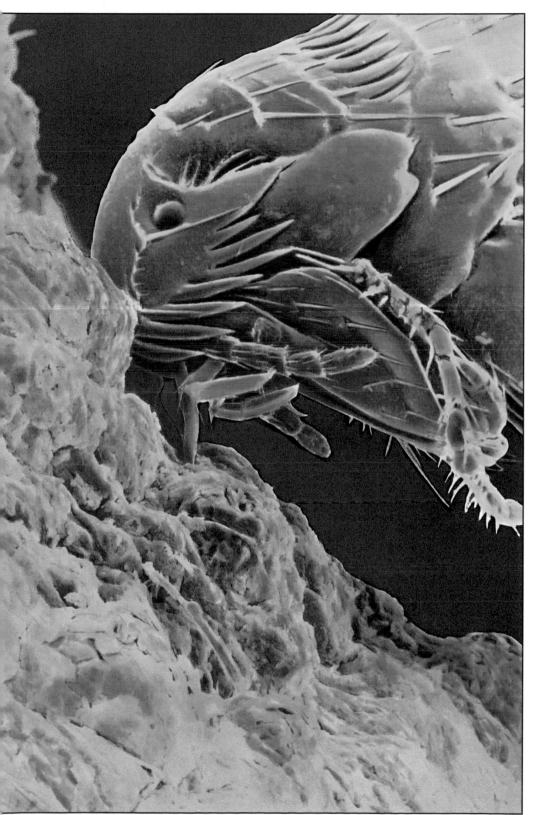

A cat flea plunging its snout into a dog's skin to suck blood

Egg bed
Flea eggs are found anywhere their host rests – indoors in a pet's bed, or outdoors in moist sand or grit, perhaps in a pet's favourite resting place under a shrub.

How big?
Flea eggs are very small – only about 0.5 mm across. You could probably fit two of them on the head of a pin. Flea larvae are a bit bigger – between 1–2 mm long.

I am a female flea. After mating with a male flea, I start to lay eggs. I need to be well fed and contented to do this, so I begin right after a meal. My eggs are pearly white and so small they are next to impossible to see. Usually I lay two or three a day. I place them loosely in the fur so they can drop into the place where my host is resting.

After a week or so, my eggs hatch out as little worms called larvae.

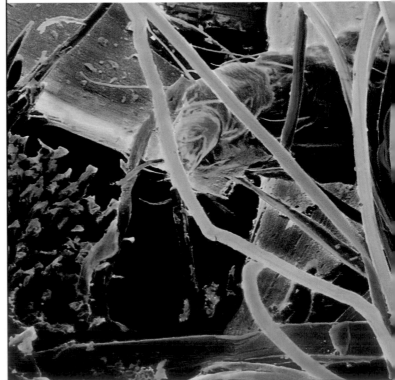

Flea larvae are blind and they avoid light. They skulk in dark cracks and feed on any odd scraps they find – dead flakes of skin, hair and the nutritious blood droppings that rain down from us feeding adults.

My offspring will probably spend the whole winter as larvae before they spin silky cocoons and turn into adults as the weather gets warmer.

Cocoon
Flea cocoons often look like dusty balls filled with carpet fluff, hairs and flakes of skin.

Human skin flakes

A flea larva lurking in the fibres of a carpet

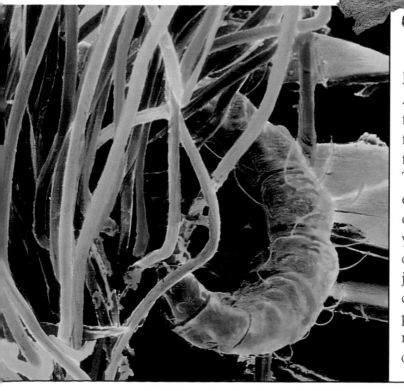

Hidden family
Adult biting fleas make up five percent of fleas in a home. The rest will be eggs, larvae or cocoons. So if you or your pets are bitten by just five fleas a day, there are probably 95 more hidden out of sight.

19

Don't breathe
A flea can stay in its cocoon for up to a year. But it pops out as soon as it senses the heat, vibrations, noise, or even the breath, of a warm-blooded animal.

Cats and dogs
About 95% of the fleas on cats and dogs in the United States are cat fleas, while pets in Europe mainly have dog fleas.

In the right conditions, our eggs can turn into adults in ten days. It is possible for me and just nine other healthy females to have your home swarming with over 100,000 eggs, larvae, cocoons and adults within 30 days if the weather is warm and humid.

The most likely time for us to attack is when you and your pets come back from a holiday. While you were away, all the eggs the adult fleas had laid were busy hatching out into larvae and the larvae were becoming cocoons.

The cocoons wait patiently for warm-blooded hosts to turn up. The moment a family walks in the door, every flea in the place will know about it and get set to jump aboard.

Under attack
The worst time for humans to get bitten is when infested pets go away. Newly hatched fleas will now turn on people, although they cannot lay eggs on a diet of human blood.

House check
One way to check for fleas is to wear white socks on a carpet that has not been walked on for several days. If more than five fleas show up on your feet and ankles, you have a serious flea problem.

Before feeding

After feeding

Little vampire
A bed bug can take in six times its weight in blood at a single meal. That's like you eating about 180 kg of food in one go.

Stink bug
Bed bugs have strong scent glands. When a bed bug is frightened, it leaks an oily liquid with a disgusting, sweetish stink – some say like rotting raspberries.

Night raiders

I am a bed bug. I got my name because I like to live either near or in a human's bed. During the day I hide out in any dark crevice I can find – in floorboards, bed frames, alarm clocks, even the seams of a mattress.

At night, I wake up to hunt for a meal. My favourite food is human blood. I head toward the warmth of the nearest sleeping body and crawl up and down until I come across a patch of bare flesh.

Once I find a promising site I ease my sharp beak into the skin. Then, using it like a straw, I take a long drink of warm blood. To make sure my beak doesn't get blocked, I inject a drop of saliva into the hole to keep the blood flowing steadily.

I can suck for up to 12 minutes before I drop off my host as bloated as a balloon.

When I've finished my meal, I stagger to my hiding place for a few days to digest the feast.

Most humans don't feel a thing while I'm feeding on them. When my host wakes the next morning, all he notices is a hard round welt on his skin that itches like mad where his body has reacted to my saliva.

Big bugs
Bed bugs are only about 5 mm long, but they are too big to fit on the head of a pin.

The bed bug uses its long feelers to "smell" the air as it searches for blood.

Bed bug diet
In cold places,
a bed bug can
last for 500
days without a
drop of blood
to drink. But it
would not
lay eggs during
that time.

**No wings –
can't fly**
Bed bugs can't
fly. They can
only crawl. So a
good way to
stop them from
spreading is to
wrap double-
sided sticky
tape around the
legs of beds.

You look pale
A newly
hatched bed
bug, or nymph,
is a pale straw
colour. But it
turns deep red
or purple after
its first meal
of blood.

Recently, I found myself on
an empty bed. But I'm not worried.
If I have to, I can wait more than
six months for my next meal
of blood.

In the meantime, since there is
nothing to disturb me, I will lay
some eggs. Usually, I produce a few
dozen at a time. The eggs are
covered with sticky glue that fastens
them firmly to the rough surfaces of
the cracks and crevices in which I
place them. This keeps them from
rolling away. After about two weeks,
the eggs will hatch out as small,
almost colourless versions of me
and my mate. It will then take a
couple of months for my brood
to become fully grown.

If my family here ever runs out of humans, we will have to find new hosts. We bed bugs can move fast and far when we need to. We might explore along pipes to get into the homes next door, or we might hitch a ride in furniture and move to a new place altogether. We might even climb aboard passing pets or wild birds if there are no handy humans around. During the eighteen months that is our life span, we can go a pretty long way in search of new hosts.

Not fussy
If there are no human victims, bed bugs may attack guinea pigs, rabbits, rats, bats, birds and chickens.

Bed bugs of all ages – adults, youngsters, babies and eggs

Itch mites are
0.5 mm long.
About two of
them could fit
onto the head
of a pin.

*Cross-section of
human skin showing
a burrowing itch
mite under the
surface*

I am a a female itch mite – a
cousin of the dust mites. Instead of
eating skin flakes, we itch mites
burrow right into human skin! The
good news is that male itch mites
stay on the surface and do little harm.
The bad news is that we females are
great diggers and can
spread from person to
person like wildfire.

We use our mouth and front legs to bite into skin cells and suck out the fluid inside. We don't go deeper than the outer layers of skin – that's why no blood comes gushing out – but our burrows can wind along for more than 2.5 cm. A burrow isn't much wider than a hair, so it's nearly impossible for humans to see. What they can't miss, though, is the itchy rash we give them.

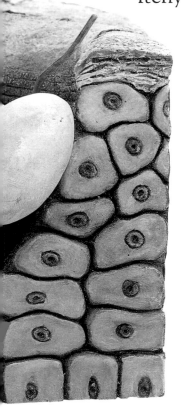

As we dig, we lay eggs, usually about three a day. After eight weeks and more than 150 eggs, we die. Within three or four days the eggs hatch out and baby mites climb to the surface, where they live until they start to lay eggs themselves.

Sore and itchy
Chemicals from the mite's body irritate the skin it digs in. This causes scabies, a disease that makes skin sore and itchy and covers it in bumps, blisters and sores.

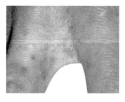

Find the fold
Itch mites like to dig in folds of the skin at the fingers, armpits, wrists, groin and legs.

People carriers
Itch mites live only on humans, and scabies spreads easily. All it takes is for one infected person to shake hands with someone.

I am an eyelash mite. Imagine being as small as me and living on a great, big, blinking eyelash. Whenever the eyelids flutter, I go up and down, up and down. It's like living on a giant fairground ride!

We eyelash mites are really small – much smaller than our itch mite cousins – and we are colourless, too. So if you haven't got a very powerful microscope, don't even try to look for us – it's impossible. But if you did look at us through a microscope you would see a cigar-shaped body and four pairs of legs. These are the only features that give us away.

For most of our lives, we live harmlessly in the socket, or follicle, of an eyelash.

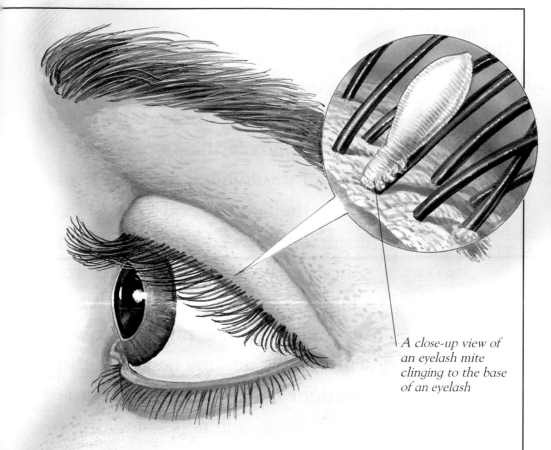

A close-up view of an eyelash mite clinging to the base of an eyelash

We hang on to the lash, a bit like a caterpillar hangs on to a tree, but always pointing head down so we can suck up the juices that ooze out of human skin.

Because we don't burrow into skin, we don't have any serious ill effects on people. And because we are invisible, nobody really takes much notice of us at all.

Day and night
Eyelash mites spend their days feeding within a hair follicle. At night they come up to the skin's surface to mate.

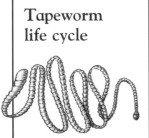

1. A human eats meat infected by a bladderworm, which develops into an adult tapeworm.

2. The adult tapeworm produces eggs, which are released in human faeces.

3. The eggs are eaten by an animal and hatch into larvae.

4. Larvae enter the animal's muscles and become cysts (bladderworms).

My body is a chain of flat segments, strung together like the box cars on a freight train. As I grow, new segments appear from my neck. Each segment is both male and female, so I can fertilize myself and produce eggs without a mate.

Once a segment of my body fills up with eggs, it drops off and passes out of my host. If these eggs are swallowed by a grazing animal, they will hatch out inside it as larvae.

Once the larvae have hatched, they will burrow through the animal's intestines and into its bloodstream. Then they will drift to other parts of its body, such as the organs and muscles. Here, they will form cysts, or new bladderworms.

If humans eat the animal's flesh without cooking it properly first, the bladderworms will turn into tapeworms inside their intestines and the cycle will begin again.

New segments are produced from behind the head.

A tapeworm's body can be very long, but it is seldom more than 1 cm wide.

Need a host
Tapeworms are parasites. A parasite is an animal that can only live on or inside another animal – the host. Without a host, a parasite cannot survive.

Each segment contains both male and female sex organs.

One ripe segment can contain about 100,000 eggs!

Quick cure
A single dose of drugs will get rid of a tapeworm living inside a person's intestines.

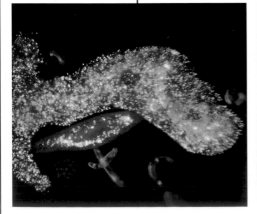

Amoeba in action

I'm tiny – incredibly tiny. In fact, I am one of the smallest complete bundles of life possible – just a single, soft, squishy cell. Cells are the little building blocks that living beings are made of. Your body is made of billions of cells that work together to keep you alive. But I don't need other cells to keep me going. I have no head, legs, or fins, but I can move, eat and even think for myself.

When I want to find food, I slowly slide a false foot forward.

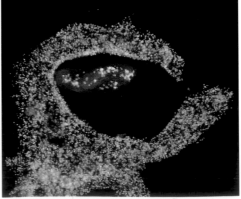

1. The amoeba moves toward its meal and spreads its blobby body around it.

2. The amoeba starts to encircle its prey with its body.

It is called a false foot because it is actually just a branch of my body. I use my foot to probe what's out there. If it hits a bacteria, algae or something else I can eat, I flow after it as fast I can. Like a tiny blob of treacle, I spread out so my body completely surrounds the food particle. Then I pour in digestive juices until the food is dissolved and can be absorbed by my body.

We amoebas may be slow, but we have had hundreds of millions of years to spread around the world. I've got cousins, for example, who live only in the sea and others who live only in ponds and lakes. Some even survive as parasites in the bodies of bigger animals.

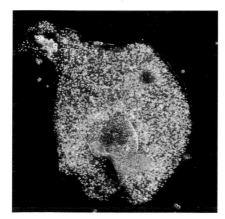

3. Once it has surrounded its prey, the amoeba digests its meal.

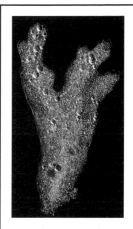

Mighty small
This picture shows an amoeba 40 times bigger than it is in real life. If you were 40 times bigger, you would be nearly twice as big as a blue whale – the largest animal in the world.

Hard times
If food or water runs out, amoebas form a tough layer on their surface and become resting cysts. When things get better, they wake up and start to move again.

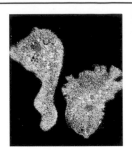

Divide and multiply
When amoebas reproduce they simply divide into two equal (but smaller) halves. These offspring are usually called daughter amoebas.

Lots of us amoebas do no harm at all if we invade the bodies of bigger animals. A few amoebas, though, are really dangerous. They can cause illnesses such as dysentery in humans. Dysentery is a disease that sends people running to the toilet every few minutes until they get so weak they collapse. In fact, amoebic dysentery can kill if it isn't treated quickly.

This amoeba is about to surround another amoeba before eating it

False foot

Dysentery is spread by food and water contaminated by the dysentery amoeba. This amoeba thrives wherever there are open sewers, or where raw sewage is used to fertilize crops.

When amoebas infect food and water, and then get swallowed, they make themselves at home in the human gut. The trouble starts once they invade the walls of the intestines. There they cause terrible pains and trigger bouts of dysentery. It takes several different medicines to cure the illness, although washing hands well and making sure water is pure is probably the best way to keep this disease at bay.

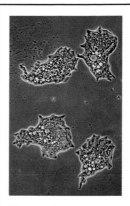

Fast change
It takes less than an hour for a parent amoeba to turn itself into a pair of amoeba offspring.

Movie monster
In the movie *The Blob*, filmmakers used the idea of an amoeba to create a giant blobby monster that engulfed its victims and swallowed them whole.

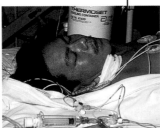

The king of fever

I'm deadly and I'm proud! I am a mighty single-cell parasite called Plasmodium. My ancestors and I have attacked probably half the human beings who ever lived.

Today we kill two to three million people a year with a dreaded disease called malaria.

What makes us parasites? The only places we can live are in the blood and liver cells of human beings and in the stomach cells of one particular kind of mosquito. Put us anywhere else and we'll die.

We live in the tropics and in warmer regions where our mosquito hosts breed.

Once we get into a person we start to eat the contents of the red blood cells (the cells that carry oxygen from the lungs to the rest of the body). This makes our victims so weak that they eventually die. Fortunately, the person usually dies slowly enough for other mosquitoes to take a sip of infected blood. That's how we get passed onto other humans.

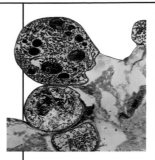

Tiny terror
Although a Plasmodium causes huge problems, it is a tiny organism. The picture above has been magnified about 500 times.

Lucky find
It was only a century ago that Ronald Ross, an English doctor working in India, discovered that it was a biting mosquito that passed malaria from human to human.

Could be 'flu
Early signs of malaria feel like 'flu, though a simple blood test can tell which is which. Malaria has to be treated early if victims are to survive.

At the moment, I am sitting in a mosquito's saliva gland with hundreds of my brothers and sisters. Our parents were living in the blood of a human malaria victim. When this mosquito drank the human's blood, she sucked up our parents too. They hurried to her stomach cells, where they started to breed and produce us. We swarmed into this saliva gland, ready to flow down the mosquito's mouthparts when she takes her next meal of human blood.

As she feeds, she will inject us into her victim. We will hitch a ride through the human's bloodstream to get to the liver, where we'll rest and multiply for a while.

Then we will plunge into the bloodstream again and start feeding on the human's red blood cells. I will enter a cell, eat up its contents, and produce lots of offspring – so many that the walls of the cell will burst.

Feelers covered in sensitive hairs help the mosquito to find her host.

Human hairs are not always sensitive enough to warn humans that they are being bitten by a mosquito.

The mouthparts have sensors at the tip to let the mosquito know she has reached the right host.

A swarm of new parasites (16 times stronger than before) will escape, ready to eat more blood cells.

The poisonous waste I produce while feeding will also be released. These poisons will cause the hot fevers of malaria in our victim.

Meanwhile, the next female mosquito to come along for a drink will suck in a gut full of us parasites. We will head for her stomach, eager to start the whole cycle again.

Mild males
This male mosquito is harmless. Only the females drink blood. The males stick to fruit juice and plant sap.

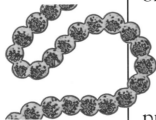

Billions of bacteria

You cough. You moan. Your throat feels raw as if a razor is cutting into it. You've caught a bug and ... that's where I come in.

I'm a bacteria, the smallest form of life on earth. More exactly, I am a streptococcus bacteria (you can call me strep). I'm so small I'm invisible, but I pack a terrific punch if I infect someone's throat. Once I get in, I multiply like mad in the wet warmth. By the end of just one day, there may be hundreds of millions of bacteria lining the walls of the throat.

Humans react violently to me and my family. They come down with a painful

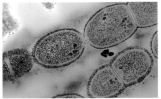

Streptococci bacteria growing on human tonsils

illness known as strep throat. The inside of the gullet turns an angry red colour.

Hair-like threads help this bacteria to move around.

A slimy outer layer keeps the bacteria from drying out.

It becomes dotted with specks of pus. Glands in the neck swell up and become tender. Soon swallowing hurts so badly it is almost impossible to eat. Fever, chills, headaches and stomach aches pile on the misery. Even with medical attention, people stay sick anywhere from three to five days.

Smallest of all
Bacteria are so small that about 1,000 could fit on the head of a pin.

Not likely
Only one child in ten with a sore throat and fever can blame it on strep bacteria.
The other nine children can blame it on viral infections.

Born free
While still in its mother's womb, a human baby is completely free of bacteria. But the instant babies are born, they start to acquire billions of bacteria. From then on, humans are like walking gardens of bacteria.

Billions
The human body has more bacteria than it has cells. Many cluster on the skin. Others line the mouth and nose. Still more live in the intestines, where they help to keep humans healthy.

Fortunately, I am a mild bacteria. It is easy to get rid of me using antibiotics – drugs that help the human body fight off bacteria. But I have relatives who are real thugs and can do nasty things to humans.

My cousins E.coli are common bacteria that live in animal intestines. There they stop other harmful bacteria from growing and help to make important vitamins. But one rare strain of the family is a brute. It can wreck the lining of the intestine and cause terrible cramps, diarrhoea and vomiting. It is mostly picked up by people who have eaten undercooked infected meat.

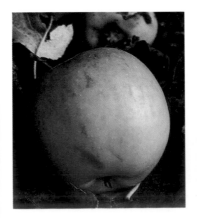

But please don't get me wrong. Not all of us bacteria are bad. Some of us do a lot of good.

For example, soil is packed with all kinds of bacteria. Many of us spend our time recycling animal dung or making sure dead creatures and plants rot. We can help to keep a field of cows healthy by working with dung beetles to break down the cows' dung and turning it into mulch to enrich the soil.

If we bacteria didn't do our job, dead plants and animals would litter the landscape forever.

These photographs show an apple rotting. Once an apple is damaged, it is infected with bacteria that break down its cells.

Simple shapes
Bacteria belong to four main groups: the round beaded types (called cocci), short rods (called bacilli), bent rods (called vibrios) and spiral shapes (called spirilla).

Glossary

Allergic
To suffer a bad reaction to a substance that is usually harmless.

Antibiotic drugs
Drugs that stop the growth of or destroy living things that cause diseases in animals.

Beak
A bug's long, sharp mouthparts.

Bladderworm
The stage in a tapeworm's life after it hatches from its egg.

Cell
The building blocks that make up all living things.

Cocoon
The soft casing in which a larva develops into the next stage of its life.

Contaminate
To infect something by touching it or mixing with it.

Cyst
The outer covering of a living thing in a resting stage of its development.

Digestive juices
Liquid filled with chemicals that help to break down food so that it can be absorbed by a plant or animal.

Dysentery
A sickness caused by a particular amoeba.

Faeces
Solid waste or droppings that pass out of animals.

Follicle
The socket from which a hair grows.

Glands
Structures inside a plant or animal that produce chemicals such as digestive juices.

Gullet
The tube inside the neck that takes food from the mouth to the stomach.

Host
A living thing on which other living things feed.

Infect
To pass on or spread a disease.

Infest
To swarm or attack in a troublesome way.

Intestines
The tubes inside the body that digest and absorb food and water.

Larva
A young animal that is completely different from an adult animal of the same kind. For example, a caterpillar is the larva of a butterfly.

Liver
An organ in the body that produces chemicals to break down fatty food.

Microscope
An instrument for looking at tiny things. It has lenses that make things look bigger.

Nest
A place where an animal sleeps and rears its young.

Nit
A louse's egg.

Nucleus
A structure inside a cell that tells the cell what to do.

Nymph
A young, partly developed insect.

Parasite
A living being that can only survive by living on or in another living being.

Red blood cells
Blood cells that carry oxygen around the body.

Snout
A nose that sticks out of a creature's head.

Vitamins
Substances that an animal needs in order for its body to grow and work well.

Warm-blooded animal
Animals whose bodies stay at a constant warm temperature. All birds and mammals are warm-blooded animals.